Happiness

By Marcia & Dave Kaplan

*The material in this book has
been compiled over a long period
of time. Many of the sources are
unknown to the compilers. We wish
to acknowledge the original
authors whoever they may be.*

*Cover Art: Bill Stevens
Inside Art: Phil Mendez & Duffy Doland*

ISBN: 0-9617744-3-6

Happiness is good.
The place to be happy is here.
The time to be happy is now.
The way to be happy is to help
make others happy.

Happiness can be caught, sought or thought, but never bought;
The best way to keep happiness is to share it.

Considering all of the things you wear, your expression is the most important.

Happiness is not created by what happens to us, but by our attitudes toward each happening.

...Walter Heily

It isn't our position but our disposition which makes us happy.

Co-operation is spelled with two letters — WE!

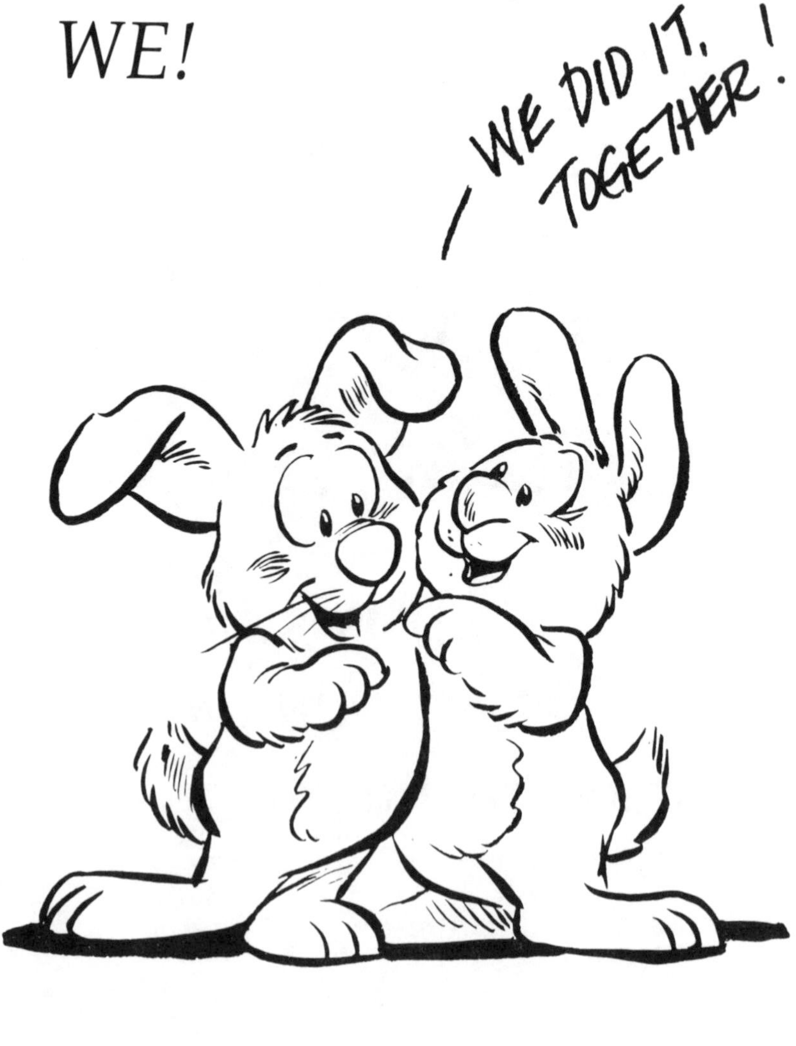

The surest way to knock the chip off a fellow's shoulder is by patting him on the back.

*It is fine to aim high
if we have developed the
ability to accomplish our
aims, but there is no use
aiming unless the gun is
loaded.*

William Ross

Stopping at third base adds nothing to the score.

That lucky rabbit's foot didn't work for the rabbit.

Set your eyes on the stars, yet keep your feet on the ground.

If you don't stick your neck out, you'll never get your head above the crowd.

*Even a woodpecker
owes his success
to the fact that
he uses his head.*

...M. Pratt

*Anywhere is paradise;
it's up to you.*

*May the next
brilliant face
you see be yours.*

*Two little words
that make the
difference —
Start Now!*

*A foot in the
door is worth two
on the desk.*

*The more chance there
is of stubbing your toe,
the more chance you have
of stepping into success.*

People willing to roll up their sleeves seldom lose their shirts.

A man who is pulling his own weight never has any left to throw around.

The middle of the road is where the white line is — and that's the worst place to drive.

...Robert Frost

Happiness is a slice of life —
Buttered!

...*Al Bernstein*

*Happiness is a rainbow
in your heart.*

What sunshine is to flowers, smiles are to humanity.

...Addison

*Cheerfulness is what
greases the axles of
the world.
Don't go through life
creaking.*

...H.W. Byles

The problem is not the problem. The problem is one's attitude about the problem.

Swallowing your pride occasionally will never give you indigestion.

A person who wins may have been counted out several times, but didn't hear the referee.

Success is that old A B C...
Ability, Brawn and Courage.

Patience is the ability to count down before you blast off.

To handle yourself,
use your head;
To handle others,
use your heart.

It is always too soon to quit.

*If you think you can
or you think you can't...*

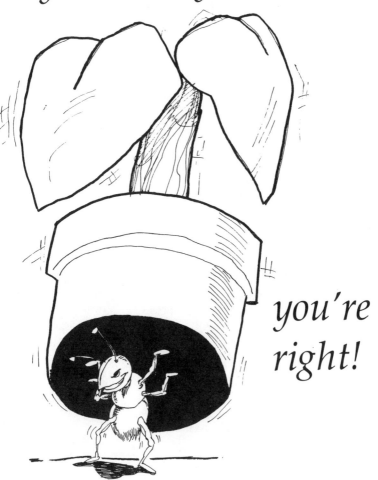

*you're
right!*

There is no "I" in teamwork.

*People who complain
about the way the
ball bounces are
usually the ones
who dropped it.*

*Watch the little things;
a small leak will sink
a great ship.*

…Benjamin Franklin

Plan ahead…
It wasn't raining
when Noah built the ark.

Oversleeping won't make your dreams come true.

*It is easier to go down a
hill than up, but the view
is best from the top.*

...*Arnold Bennett*

Practice an attitude of gratitude.

Friendship is like vitamins; we supplement each other's minimum daily requirements.

...Kathy Mohnke

The world is divided into people who do things and people who get the credit. Try, if you can, to belong to the first class. There's far less competition.

...Dwight Morrow

We can't all be heros
because someone has to
sit on the curb and
clap as they go by.

...Will Rogers

Attitudes are contagious! Is yours worth catching?

Jumping for joy is good exercise.

HAPPINESS IS WITHIN

It's not so much the world outside
That makes us laugh or smile;
It's more the thoughts within our hearts
That make life seem worthwhile.

...Wisconsin Odd Fellow

You're never too old to become younger.

Triumph is just the extra "UMPH" added to the "TRY" !

The dictionary is the only place where **success** comes before **work.**

Every man has an equal chance to become better than he is.

Life consists not in holding good cards, but in playing those you do hold well.

...Josh Billings

A smile is a frown turned upside-down.

*The world is round,
and the place which
may seem like the end
may also be only the
beginning.*

...Ivy Baker Priest

*God gives every bird
its food; but does not
throw it into the nest.*

...Hoffand

Success is a ladder that cannot be climbed with your hands in your pockets.

There is always a little boy in the old man gone fishing.

...J. Calder Joseph

You say there is no such thing as luck. Well, what about doing what you enjoy best and making a living at it?

...Arnold Glasow

The gem cannot be polished without friction nor man without trials.

...Confucius

It takes both rain and sunshine to make a rainbow.

There is a vast difference between hopeless end and endless hope.

*Being in a good
frame of mind
helps keep one in
the picture of health.*

*The finest inheritance
you can give your children
is to allow them to make
their own way, completely
on their own feet.*

Happiness is something to do, something to love, and something to hope for.

No symphony orchestra ever played music like a two year old girl laughing with her puppy.

...Bern Williams

Imagination is only intelligence having fun.

...George Scialabbe

In spite of the cost of living, it's still popular.

...Kathleen Norris

Everybody needs a hug.
It changes your metabolism.

...Leo Buscaglia

Kindness, like a boomerang, always returns.

Autumn is a second spring when every leaf is a flower.

*Our eyes are placed
in front because
it is more important
to look ahead than back.*

Past experience should be a guide post, not a hitching post.

You can give without loving, but you can never love without giving.

Happiness held is
the seed;
Happiness shared is
the flower.

One machine can do the work of fifty ordinary men.

No machine can do the work of one extraordinary man.

...Elbert Hubbard

Motivation is when your dreams put on work clothes.

...Parts Pups

Happiness is excitement that has found a settling down place.

But there is always a little corner that keeps flapping around.

...E.L. Konigsburg

Laughter is a tranquilizer with no side effects.

…Arnold Glasow

It isn't what you know that counts, its what you think of in time.

You can avoid having
ulcers by adapting to
the situation:
If you fall in the
mud puddle, check
your pockets for
fish.

Wear a smile —
One size fits all.

…Orben's Current Comedy

Your most important sale is to sell yourself to yourself.

*Ideas are like apples;
to get them you have
to shake the tree.*

*When you reach for the stars,
you may not quite get one;
but, you won't come up with
a handful of mud either.*

*People judge you
by your actions,
not by your intentions.
You may have a heart
of gold, but so does
a hard boiled egg.*

…Good Reading

Luck has a peculiar habit of favoring those who don't depend on it.

Most people are about as happy as they make up their minds to be.

...*Abraham Lincoln*

MAY YOU HAVE

Enough happiness to keep you sweet,
Enough trials to keep you strong,
Enough sorrow to keep you human,
Enough hope to keep you happy,
Enough failure to keep you humble,
Enough success to keep you eager,
Enough friends to give you comfort,
Enough wealth to meet your needs,
Enough enthusiasm to look forward,
Enough faith to banish depression,
Enough.determination to make each day
    better than yesterday.

                    ...Anonymous

Happiness sneaks in through a door you didn't know you left open.

...John Barrymore

*Wishing you Good Health,
Good Luck, Good Times,
Good Friends, and Happiness
that never ends.*

USE THIS CONVENIENT ORDER FORM FOR ADDITIONAL
COPIES OF ALL THE KAPLAN BOOKS

NAME _____

ADDRESS _____

CITY _____

STATE _____ ZIP CODE _____

I WOULD LIKE TO ORDER:

_____ CHEERS BOOKS @ $6.95

_____ SMILES BOOKS @ $6.95

_____ FRIENDS BOOKS @ $6.95

_____ HAPPINESS BOOKS @ $6.95

_____ THANKS BOOKS @ $6.95

_____ KINDNESS BOOKS @ $6.95

_____ 3 BOOK SETS WITH SLIP COVER @ $21.00
          (CHEERS, SMILES, FRIENDS)

PLEASE SEND ORDER FORM AND CHECK OR MONEY ORDER
TO: **CHEERS, P.O. BOX 550513, ATLANTA, GA. 30355-3013**

PAYMENT ACCEPTED IN U.S. DOLLARS ONLY.

USE THIS CONVENIENT ORDER FORM FOR ADDITIONAL
COPIES OF ALL THE KAPLAN BOOKS

NAME _____

ADDRESS _____

CITY _____

STATE _____ ZIP CODE _____

I WOULD LIKE TO ORDER:

_____ CHEERS BOOKS @ $6.95

_____ SMILES BOOKS @ $6.95

_____ FRIENDS BOOKS @ $6.95

_____ HAPPINESS BOOKS @ $6.95

_____ THANKS BOOKS @ $6.95

_____ KINDNESS BOOKS @ $6.95

_____ 3 BOOK SETS WITH SLIP COVER @ $21.00
          (CHEERS, SMILES, FRIENDS)

PLEASE SEND ORDER FORM AND CHECK OR MONEY ORDER
TO: **CHEERS, P.O. BOX 550513, ATLANTA, GA. 30355-3013**

PAYMENT ACCEPTED IN U.S. DOLLARS ONLY.